The Chris
Guide to Relationships

The Christian Teen's Guide to Relationships

*

Exploring Issues and Answers for Healthy Relationships

Written by: Roderick Levi Evans

Abundant Truth PUBLISHING
abundantpublishing.net
P.O. Box 126, Camden, NC 27921

The Christian Teen's Guide to Relationships
Exploring Issues and Answers for Healthy Relationships

Front & Back Cover Designs by Abundant Truth Publishing

Abundant Truth Publishing
an imprint of Abundant Truth International Ministries

For information address:
Abundant Truth International
P.O. Box 126
Camden, NC 27921

Unless otherwise indicated, all of the scripture quotations are taken from the *Authorized King James Version* **of the Bible. Scripture quotations marked with NIV are taken from the** *New International Version* **of the Bible. Scripture quotations marked with ASV are taken from the** *American Standard Version* **of the Bible. Scripture quotations marked with GW are taken from the** *God's Word Bible***.**

ISBN 13: 978-1-60141-145-7

Printed in the United States of America.

Contents

Contents *(cont.)*

Introduction

Numerous challenges face today's youth. Young people have to make tough decisions daily. No matter what race, ethnicity, social status, or gender; teens and youth are surrounded by various negative and positive influences.

Because of this, the Christian Teens and Youths have a hard task before them. They have to maintain proper Christian character and conduct while they develop as individuals.

Though the challenge is great, God offers answers and practical insights through the Word of God and the wisdom of the Spirit; that even teens can represent Christ in faithfulness in spite of their ages.

In this book, we will discuss relationships and the Christian teen. The first area that we will consider is friendships. The Christian teen will discover how to have positive and wholesome friendships. They will learn strategies for dissolving bad friendships.

The second area that we will explore is the "dating" relationship. Christian teens will learn to set boundaries for their interactions in order to maintain a proper relationship with God. In addition, they will learn to be honest about their feelings and temptations and abort any relationship that will have a negative impact on their future successes. The Christian youth will understand how to have fruitful, peaceful, and beneficial relationships in his/her life.

~Part 1~

FRIENDSHIPS

Roderick Levi. Evans

Friendships and the

Christian Teen

Choosing friends can be difficult for anyone regardless of age, gender, or race. This is especially true of the Christian Teen. They are continually instructed by family, church members, and others about whom they should and should not be with.

Sometimes, it may seem as if people do not understand where you are coming from or going through in this area. However, your relationship with God can be a source of strength and comfort in choosing friends. In this section, we want to discuss the Christian teen and his/her friends.

THE MOST IMPORTANT FRIENDSHIP

Before discussing, in detail, friendships and the Christian teen, we want to talk about the closest friend that a teen will have. No other friendship can take the place of the one that you can have with Christ.

Through the scriptures and inspiration of the Spirit, we learn of Christ's love and loyalty to us. He serves as the ultimate example of a friend. Before the Christian teen can form truly lasting, healthy friendships, a solid friendship with the Lord should be formed.

Ye are my friends, if ye do whatsoever

I command you. (John 15:14)

Jesus called the apostles His friends. Because you now have received Him, you become His friend. However, to be a true friend of Christ, we have to do what He instructs us to do in the Word or by inspiration of His Spirit.

As a Christian teen, you should be willing to follow Him because His commands come to bless and prosper you, if obeyed. You establish your relationship with Christ not only through prayer and Bible Study, but through obedience.

If you are walking with Christ in obedience, you will not be vulnerable to bad friendships that may hinder you rather than help you. The Christian teen has to remember that regardless of any other friendships; his/her friendship with the Lord is the most important one.

Q & A CONCERNING FRIENDSHIPS

There are many issues facing Christian teens and youth and friends. To feel accepted, liked, and loved is important to teens and youth. The Christian teen has an added responsibility in choosing the right friends.

Because this issue is broad, this section is set up in the form of questions and answers. This will help the Christian teen to make the right decisions in friendships.

1. Can I have friends who are not Christians or unsaved?

Yes. However, your interaction with them has to come with limitations. Do not allow yourself to think that in order to witness to them or win them to Christ, you have to show them you are approachable in an ungodly manner.

You do not have to compromise your integrity to win someone to Christ. Sin and compromise has never won anyone to Christ. Even though Christ ate with sinners, He did not perform ungodly acts, engage in ungodly conversations, or go into places of sin.

Roderick Levi. Evans

But as he which hath called you is holy, so be ye holy in all manner of conversation. (I Peter 1:15)

Christian teens have tried drugs, sex, going to clubs, fighting, and other ungodly acts trying to prove that they understand where their friends are. It sounds strange, but some have done it, claiming that God wanted them to do it.

As a Christian teen, you should never agree to go to an ungodly activity or engage in something that is ungodly or wrong in order to get someone to come to church with you or listen to you. This is a trap.

2. Do I have to give up my friends who are Christian and doing some things that are not Christ-like?

While it is true that all have sinned, your relationship with other Christian teens that are practicing wrong acts also has to be put on limitation. In the Bible, Paul told believers that if someone was operating frequently or consistently in an area of sin, they were not to eat with them.

> *But now I have written unto you not to keep company, if any man that is called a brother be a fornicator, or covetous, or an idolater, or a railer, or a drunkard, or an extortioner; with such an one no not*

eat. (I Corinthians 5:11)

Eating has always been a sign of fellowship. They may be a brother or sister. However, if they are continually walking contrary to God's words, your interaction with them has to diminish. This does not mean that you do not talk to them or try to encourage them.

It implies that you withdraw some fellowship as a sign that you are not in agreement with their activity. In addition, you should pray for them that God would bless, help, and restore them. Consider the following:

Brethren, if a man be overtaken in a fault, ye which are spiritual, restore such an one in the spirit of meekness; considering thyself, lest thou also be tempted. (Galatians 6:1)

Never try to help anyone alone if you are spiritually unable to do so. There may be the possibility of you falling in the same areas (especially areas of a sexual nature.) However, you can lead them to someone who has the right information and inspiration for their situation.

If any man see his brother sin a sin which is not unto death, he shall ask, and he shall give him life for them that sin not unto death. (I John 5:16)

If you see your brother or sister in sin,

pray for them. Even if you feel they will not listen to you, pray that God will open up their hearts and change their minds.

> *Brethren, if any of you do err from the truth, and one convert him; Let him know, that he which converted the sinner from the error of his way shall save a soul from death and shall hide a multitude of sins. (James 5:19-20)*

James tells us that we should strive for the restoration of the brother or sister. In doing so, we will save them from both spiritual (and sometimes natural) death.

3. Can I hang out with friends who are

doing things that are wrong, even if I know I will not do any of those things?

Though it is possible to do that, it is not beneficial, nor does it give the proper view of a Christian. If you are a Christian, ungodly environments should not be attractive to you, even if friends are there.

You would not jump into water full of dangerous sharks because your friends are in the water and seem to enjoy it.

Likewise, you should not place yourself in an where you are surrounded by ungodly acts such as lewd dancing, sexual activity, drinking, wild partying, and smoking.

Roderick Levi. Evans

It provides sources of temptation.

Be not deceived: evil communications corrupt good manners. (I Corinthians 15:33)

Paul told the believers not to be deceived. He said if we continue in evil communications (all manner of living), it will corrupt us. If you are a Christian, you should not want to place yourself in situations that will hinder you or your witness for Christ.

WARNING SIGNS OF BAD FRIENDSHIPS

Christian teens have to be able to recognize when they are in the wrong friendships. In this section, we have listed a number of warning signs indicating that the friendship is unfruitful or unhealthy.

1. Your friends (saved or unsaved) practice sin and are comfortable.

Because you are a Christian, there should be no fellowship or agreement with ungodliness and those who practice it.

Be ye not unequally yoked together with unbelievers: for what fellowship hath righteousness with unrighteousness? and what communion hath light with darkness? And what concord hath Christ with Belial? or what part hath he that believeth with an infidel? And what agreement hath the temple of God with idols? for ye are the temple of the living God; as God hath said, I will dwell in them, and walk in them; and I will be God, and they shall be my people. Wherefore come out from among them, and be ye separate, saith the Lord, and touch not the unclean thing; and I will receive you. And will be a Father unto you, and ye shall be my sons and daughters, saith the Lord Almighty. (2 Corinthians 6:14-18)

Remember, because someone has areas of weakness, it does not necessarily mean they are practicing sin. All Christians have to grow in grace and in their walks with the Lord. However, those who are comfortable with their sin and express no desire to change should be separated from. This is for your own spiritual protection.

2. You cannot be yourself in the friendship.

This is something that many teens struggle with. You can be in a friendship where the individual is not practicing any sins, but they do not allow you to be yourself.

If you are in a friendship where you are put down, ridiculed, forced to have to agree, or made to feel inadequate and worthless, it is not the will of God. Do not feel you have to take negative things in order to have friends. You are complete in Christ Jesus.

And ye are complete in him, which Is the head of all principality and power. (Colossians 2:10)

Remember, do not sacrifice your self-worth or self-esteem to have a friend. God is faithful. He knows how to bring the right people into your life. Do not be afraid to be alone. He will provide you with what you need, even good friendships.

3. Your friends try to pressure you to do wrong.

If your friends tell you that you are not being a friend because you do not join them in something wrong. You are in a bad friendship.

True friends (even unsaved) will not force you to do something that you may not want to do. A friend will like and love you, even if there is a disagreement or you do not want to do something (especially if it is wrong). Solid friendships are based upon mutual respect and trust. They will even survive hardships and tests.

A friend loveth at all times, and a brother is born for adversity. (Proverbs 17:17)

4. Your friends are the source of confusion in your home.

If your friends put you against your parents and family, they may be wrong for you. God is not the author of confusion.

He is not going to send people into your life that will cause family problems and unnecessary arguments with parents and family.

For God is not the author of confusion, but of peace... (I Corinthians 14:33a)

5. Your friends are only friends as long as you are giving something to them or doing something for them.
whatever

As Christian teens, you are to do good to all men. However, your friendships should not be based on the barter system. You say, do, and give they want in order for you to receive their friendship.

6. Your friends discourage you from pursuing educational goals.

Any friends that will try to make you drop- out of school, stop studying, or being a good student are really not friends.

True friends will encourage you in whatever gifts, talents, and abilities you have even if they do not possess them.

And let us consider one another to provoke unto love and to good works. (Hebrews 10:24)

Roderick Levi. Evans

There are some teens who fail tests, drop out of school activities, leave school, and the like because of friends. Usually after the friend is gone, they regret those decisions.

7. Your friends expose you to ungodly acts and things.

Some friends will not pressure you into doing wrong. However, there are some, in spite of their knowledge of your walk with the Lord, who will try to offer things to you in a nice way.

Some Christian teens have become addicted to drugs, alcohol, sex, pornography, and even crimes because the approach was non-threatening. Beware of individuals who cover their intentions with a good non-threatening offer.

> *Behold, I send you forth as sheep in the midst of wolves: be ye therefore wise as serpents, and harmless as doves. (Matthew 10:16)*

FREEDOM FROM BAD FRIENDSHIPS

Many Christian teens know they are in bad friendships, but do not know how to walk away from them.

To end this section, we want to provide some instructions for freedom from these types of friendships.

1. Consider your walk with the Lord above their feelings.

Some teens do not want to hurt the individual's feelings. They are concerned about what the others will think of them. However, you are being unfair to yourself if you remain friends with someone that could hinder your walk with God and affect your life in a negative manner.

> *For do I now persuade men, or God? or do I seek to please men? for if I yet pleased men, I should not be the servant of Christ. (Galatians 1:10)*

2. Trust God for wisdom on what to say and do.

Some teens feel they do not know what to say or that they may not be able to say it properly. However, God will give grace and wisdom to say what has to be said in order to dissolve the harmful friendship.

> *If any of you lack wisdom, let him ask of God, that giveth to all men liberally, and upbraideth not; and it shall be given him. (James 1:5)*

3. Recognize when you do not want to let them go.

Christian teens use other excuses to remain friends with an individual because they do not want to let them go. However, the Christian teen must acknowledge this and ask Christ for strength to make the proper decision. The Christian teen has to deny himself.

> *Then said Jesus unto his disciples, If any man will come after me, let him deny himself, and take up his cross, and follow me.(Matthew 16:24)*

4. Prayerfully make new friends.

Most people do not want to be alone. This is true especially of teens. Therefore, to avoid going back into bad friendships, new ones have to be formed. Again, God is faithful and will help lead you into the right friendships.

I will instruct thee and teach thee in the way which thou shalt go: I will guide thee with mine eye. (Psalm 32: 8)

5. Strengthen your walk with Christ and other Christians.

In order to overcome bad friendships, you may not need to make new friends, but strengthen existing good friendships.

In addition to this, a strong personal walk with the Lord will help during times of transition where fear and loneliness can attack the mind and heart.

Finally, my brethren, be strong in the

Lord, and in the power of his might.
(Ephesians 6:10)

Questions:

1. Do you feel you have a strong friendship with Christ?

2. Discuss other questions you may have regarding friendship.

3. Are you currently involved in any bad friendships? What are some signs?

4. Do you find it difficult to end certain friendships? Why or Why Not?

Questions:

5. What steps are involved in ending bad friendships?

6. What are some consequences of maintaining a bad friendship?

~Part 2~

DATING

Dating and the Christian Teen

One relationship among Christian Teens that presents the greatest controversy is that of the emotional type. Some call their significant others boyfriends or girlfriends. Instead of referring to this relationship as a dating relationship, we have developed the term 'special friend.'

This term is used to define the place of the individual in the person's life against other friends and acquaintances. In addition, 'special friend' is used to present a wholesome view of the relationship.

IS IT RIGHT TO HAVE A SPECIAL FRIEND?

Is it O.K. for me to date? Depending on personal and denominational preferences, there are varying answers to this question.

However, the Christian must properly use the scriptures and seek the wisdom of the Holy Spirit for a clear answer.

Within the pages of scripture, there is no direct prohibition or ban against Christian youth dating. Yet, there are numerous scriptures that govern how the Christian interacts with others.

Because the scriptures offer no clear prohibition, some use this as an excuse to date without any proper guidelines. Rather than ask whether it is O.K. to date, one must ask, "Is it o.k. for me to date?"

> All things are lawful unto me, but all things are not expedient: all things are lawful for me, but I will not be brought under the power of any. (I Corinthians 6:12)

In his letter to the Corinthians, Paul told them that even though there are many things he could do and it not be sin, he continued by saying that all things are not fitting (expedient).

This means that just because I am allowed to do something does not mean that it is always proper for me to do it. Why?

Paul states that he did not want to be brought into bondage by anything. There are things we can do (more specifically, date) that are not sin, but can be a source of bondage and weight in our lives.

> *Wherefore seeing we also are compassed about with so great a cloud of witnesses, let us lay aside every weight, and the sin which doth so easily beset us, and let us run with patience the race that is set before us. (Hebrews 12:1)*

If having a special friend puts you in a vulnerable place in maintaining personal holiness or causes hindrances in your spiritual growth, then it may not be right for YOU. This is where some Christian youth become frustrated.

Without a solid relationship with the Lord and stable spiritual support system, teens may enter into relationships that they are not spiritually or emotionally able to handle. The following are signs that you may not be ready to have a special friend or date.

1. ***You are weak in your personal walk with the Lord.***

2. ***You want a special friend to impress others.***

3. You are easily influenced by others.

In addition to the above, it is not right for you to have a special friend (or date) against the advice or discretion of your parents and church leadership.

> *Children obey your parents in the Lord: for this is right. Honour thy father and mother; (which is the first commandment with promise;) That it may be well with thee, and thou mayest live long on the earth. (Ephesians 6:1-3)*

As a Christian teen, you are instructed to obey your parents and follow leadership. It may not be favorable, but God will bless you and keep you because of your obedience. Finally, as a Christian teen, you have to seek God's direction always as to whom you are to have a relationship with.

> *Trust in the Lord with all thine heart; and lean not unto thine own understanding. In all thy ways acknowledge him, and he shall direct thy paths. Be not wise in thine own eyes: fear the Lord and depart from evil. (Proverbs 3:5-7)*

God's direction is vital and He will never lead you wrong. If you seek His will for your life, you can escape the consequences of a bad relationship.

Roderick Levi. Evans

HOW DO I PREPARE MYSELF FOR A SPECIAL FRIEND?

If the Christian teen believes that he or she ready or can handle a special friend in their lives (and has permission), then there are certain preparatory things that should be done. If these are in place, the Christian teen will have a healthy, fruitful, and godly relationship and avoid potential pitfalls.

I. Be Prayerful

One of the most important tools to prepare for dating is prayer. Prayer will help you to recognize potential pitfalls in the future relationship.

And he spake a parable unto them to this end, that men ought always to pray, and not to faint. (Luke 18:1)

Prayer helps you to remain sensitive to God's inner direction and unction. It will also help you to remain sober-minded in the relationship.

This is to ensure that your feelings and emotions do not cloud your judgment. Remember to pray also for the one you are entering the relationship with.

II. Read the Bible Consistently

Reading the Bible will help you to set the proper boundaries in the relationship.

The word of God will help you to remain in the right relationship with the Lord.

Thy word is a lamp unto my feet, and a light unto my path. (Psalm 119:105)

In addition, the word of God should govern your actions as you interact with your special friend. Remember, Christ said that men should live by every word that proceeds from the mouth of God.

III. Seek Godly Counsel

Because judgment in relationships can be clouded by emotions, outside input can be crucial. Sometimes, Christian teens try to prove they can make their own choices and decisions. This, in turn, can lead to the wrong choices, which could have lasting consequences. Godly and wise counsel can provide protection from a potentially destructive relationship.

> *Where no counsel is, the people fall: but in the multitude of counselors, there is safety. (Proverbs 11:14)*

IV. Make Sure You Know the Person You Want as a Special Friend

Never enter into a relationship of any type prematurely. Sometimes you cannot know a person fully until there is consistent interaction with them. Make sure the individual has the same aspirations and commitment to the Lord as you do. If they do not, you will have consistent problems in the relationship.

> *Can two walk together, except they be agreed? (Amos 3:3)*

God does not want you to be involved with anyone that will hinder you or your relationship with Him. If you are a saved teen, you should never enter into any romantic relationship with someone that is an unbeliever.

Your involvement with the person may weaken your ability to witness to them. Do not set yourself up for unnecessary struggles, problems,

The Christian Teen's Guide to Relationships
Exploring Issues and Answers for Healthy Relationships | 45

pressures, and confusion.

There are other things that can be done to prepare for a special friend. The above three are the most important. They will provide a proper foundation for the relationship to be built upon.

WHAT NOW? I HAVE A SPECIAL FRIEND

How do I handle having a special friend or being in a relationship? As a Christian teen, there are certain guidelines to be followed.

These boundaries will preserve your Christian witness and integrity. They will also help you to avoid creating regrets in your life.

Some teens feel it is hard to be young and saved. However, they must remember that God gives strength to those who are in need. He does not save us to fail.

> *He giveth power to the faint; and to them that have no might he increaseth strength. (Isaiah 40:29)*

God will give you the strength and peace you need to serve Him as a Christian teen. The following are safeguards to be used.

I. Be Accountable to Someone

Being accountable helps you to protect

you from yourself. As a Christian teen, you should already be accountable to your parents about your whereabouts and activities.

Because some teens are trying to establish their independence, they may not want to share EVERYTHING with their parents. Do not let this be a downfall in your life.

Aside from family and church leaders, you should have other Christian friends whom you can allow to ask you hard questions concerning your relationship. They should be able to challenge you and keep you on track with the Lord. Here is our scripture from Proverbs again.

Where no counsel is, the people fall: but in the multitude of counselors, there is safety. (Proverbs 11:14)

Some do not like accountability because they may want to experiment and experience certain things in the relationship. This is why it was afore stated that being accountable helps you to protect you from yourself. Romantic relationships stir up various feelings, especially those of a sexual nature.

There needs to be someone in the Christian teen's life who can pray for him/her and listen to their struggles. If they do not have the answer, they should be able to direct them to someone who does.

Roderick Levi. Evans

II. Be Honest about Desires and Temptations

Having a special friend will bring you face to face with your innermost desires and temptations. If a Christian teen is not willing to be honest about what is going on the inside, he/she is destined to fall into a trap.

Behold, thou desirest truth in the inward parts: and in the hidden part thou shalt make me to know wisdom. (Psalms 51:6)

If you are honest about what you are experiencing (to yourself and God), traps and snares can be avoided. The Christian teen has to remember that he/she will never experience, feel, go through, or face anything that someone else has not. Some youth are made to feel this way. It is untrue.

> *There hath no temptation taken you but such as is common to man: but God is faithful, who will not suffer you to be tempted above that ye are able; but will with the temptation also make a way to escape, that ye may be able to bear it. (I Corinthians 10:13)*

If you are honest, you invite the Lord's assistance into your situation. Your relationship with God can remain strong and your relationship with your special friend can remain pure.

III. Set Boundaries for You and Your Special Friend

Before fully entering into a relationship or at the beginning of the relationship, boundaries for intimacy have to be set. The word of God should be consulted in this matter. The flesh will want and desires things that God has reserved for those who are married only. Certain boundaries should be non-negotiable. They are:

*No Pre-marital Sex (referred to in translations as fornication, sexual immorality).

Girls and boys were created to be attracted to one another. Therefore, feelings of attraction (even those of a sexual nature) will be experienced. However, God's prohibition must be followed.

Sex is reserved for those in marriage. Society will try to tell you that it is O.K. It is not according to the word of God. Friends will try to tell you that if you do not do it before marriage, you will not know what to do.

In addition, they will try to tell you that if you plan to get married, it is O.K. This is also untrue.

For this is the will of God, even your sanctification, that ye should abstain from fornication. (I Thessalonians 4:3)

*No Sexual Activity (also referred to in some translations as sexual immorality, uncleanness, lasciviousness, etc.)

This is where many Christian teens struggle. Touching and rubbing others in an inappropriate way or in an inappropriate place should not be practiced. (Touching private parts, sexual organs, chest, inner thighs, buttocks, breasts, and the like is not appropriate.)

Do not believe the lie. These things (may not be sex) will make your struggle to remain sexually pure hard and in many instances, lead to sex.

In addition, Christian teens should not touch

or rub themselves in an inappropriate manner. This will set them up for failure in remaining free from pre-marital sex.

> *Mortify therefore your members which are upon the earth; fornication, uncleanness, inordinate affection, evil concupiscence, and covetousness, which is idolatry. (Colossians 3:5)*

There may be some teens who have been involved in sexual activity of some kind. In these cases, extra precautions have to be put in place. It is easy to fall because of experiences.

The Christian teen has to be honest about what tempts him/her and put safeguards in place. This is because teens who have had some experience will face a greater temptation to return to old ways and habits.

Aside from boundaries for intimacy, the Christian teen and his/her special friend will have to set others. These may include places where they will go, people they interact with, the amount of time alone together, and the like.

Each relationship will differ depending on those involved. However, boundaries should be in place for personal protection. Boundaries will guard against self-deception.
IV. Fellowship with the Lord, Together in Public & Corporate Worship

It has been stated that a Christian teen should not ever enter into a relationship (especially with a special friend) with an unbeliever. You will not be able to worship God fully.

However, if you and your special friend are believers, fellowship with the Lord together will strengthen the relationship and help to avoid pitfalls.

Some teens do not invite the Lord into the relationship because of their personal desires. This leaves the door open for you to fail.

Yet, this is to be done in public and corporate settings. Personal prayer and bible study could turn into something else. Hence, corporate and public worship is a safeguard.

WHAT IF I CHOOSE THE WRONG SPECIAL FRIEND?

In this final section, we want to address two questions, "What happens if I choose the wrong special friend? and What happens if I do not prepare myself and have guidelines in the relationship?" There are number of negative consequences that could occur because of carelessness with a special friend.

The Christian teen has to understand that God will forgive his/her sin, but some of the consequences of the sin may be felt;

sometimes, for the rest of the individual's life.

The information presented is to help Christian teens avoid mistakes and sins that they may regret for the rest of their lives. The following is not an exhaustive list of consequences, but a few have been identified.

1. Relationship with Christ may be hindered or lost

The Christian will suffer spiritually for entering into or having a wrong relationship. Some teens know that they have a future ministry upon their lives. The wrong involvement could negatively affect the call of God upon their lives.

In addition, some have allowed relationships to cause them to leave the Lord and give up their salvation. Remember that your relationship with the Lord is the most important thing in your life.

2. May be hurt emotionally

If the relationship with the special friend is improper, the Christian teen may be hurt emotionally. It may hinder future relationships. Some have entered bad relationships and suffered as a result.

Their feelings are hurt, and many come

out of the relationships feeling bad about themselves.

3. May be hurt physically

Others enter the wrong relationship and may leave physically damaged. This includes males and females. There have been Christian teens who can tell of how they were injured, threatened, and stalked because of entering into the wrong relationship.

The harm does not always come from a relationship with an unbeliever. In addition, be careful of individuals with ex-special friends. The "ex" may want to harm you because of the relationship.

4. Unwanted Pregnancy

The Christian teen who fails to keep his/her relationship wholesome and godly set themselves up for unwanted consequences such as pregnancy. Having a child in one's youth brings unnecessary challenges and responsibilities to teens.

The Lord wants the Christian teen to be able to grow, mature, and live without things that could have been avoided. Do not believe that it cannot happen to you.

5. Health Problems

Teens that handle relationships with their special friends in an improper manner may set themselves up for health issues resulting from sexual activity.

Numerous diseases can be contracted (or transmitted) without sexual intercourse.

6. Problems with School, Family, and Friends

Any relationship that has a negative influence upon your school performance and family and godly social life should be avoided. Some teens (for the sake of love) may ruin the respect that others have for them.

This includes their future aspirations (college, sports, and marriage), and other relationships because of the wrong interaction with a special friend. It may not seem important at the time. However, the day may come when you will want the things that you lost because of the individual.

An individual may experience other negative consequences. However, these can be avoided if Christian teens will humble themselves before the Lord. Remember, God's instructions come to protect you, not prevent you from having fun.

If you handle the relationship with the special friend properly, you will reap the benefits. In addition, God's favor and personal peace will be yours.

Questions:

1. Do you feel it is right for Christian teens to have special friends? Why? Why Not?

2. Do you feel you are ready to have a special friend?

3. Name some signs that show you are not ready for a special friend.

4. What things can you do to prepare yourself for a special friend?

5. What can you do to maintain a proper relationship with a special friend?

Questions:

6. What are some consequences of entering into a relationship in an improper way?

7. What have you learned or discovered from this section?

Made in the USA
Monee, IL
13 April 2023

31832286R00046